Contents

From the Editors and Contributors of *Threads*
A *SewStylish* publication

This material was previously published by *Threads*.
See page 32 for Credits. All rights reserved.
First published in this format 2014

Cover Photographers: (bottom left) Scott Phillips;
(all other photos) Sloan Howard

Executive Editor, Series: Shawna Mullen
Assistant Editor, Series: Timothy Stobierski
Editorial Intern: Emma Kingsley

threads

Editor: Sarah McFarland
Executive Editor: Judith Neukam
Art Director: Rosann Berry
Special Issues Technical Editor: Carol Fresia
Associate Editor: Stephani L. Miller
Assistant Editor: Dana Finkle
Special Projects Editor: Sarah Opdahl
Senior Copy/Production Editor: Jeannine Clegg
Assistant Art Director: Gloria Melfi
Administrative Assistant: April Mohr
Seamstress: Norma Bucko

threadsmagazine.com
Executive Web Producer: Victoria North
Web Producer: Evamarie Gomez
Web Editorial Assistant: Alex Lombardi

Taunton's SewStylish (ISSN: 1935-8482) is published by
The Taunton Press Inc., Newtown, CT 06470-5506.
Telephone 203-426-8171

 **The Taunton Press**
Inspiration for hands-on living®

The Taunton Press, Inc., 63 South Main Street, PO Box 5506,
Newtown, CT 06470-5506
e-mail: tp@taunton.com

Library of Congress Cataloging-in-Publication Data in progress
ISBN: 978-1-62710-772-3

Printed in the United States of America
10 9 8 7 6 5 4 3 2 1

Cotton Shirt Quilt

Like early patchwork, which was often made from salvaged fabric, this beautiful recycled quilt grew out of a collection of old cotton shirts. Though cuffs may be worn and collars may be stained, this is the perfect project to give all of your old shirts a second, indulgent life.

Simple patchwork techniques are nearly all it takes to create this quilt. Piece the cut-up button downs, layer batting over the fabric, and line with a soft fabric. Here, an oh-so-dreamy flannel lining elevates the cozy factor of this quilt. Thrift-store shirts would work fabulously for this project, and you're bound to find plenty of cotton button-down shirts in all manner of colors. You'll have as much fun chopping up these shirts as you will sewing the quilt; and you're helping the earth by using reclaimed garments. What could be better?

RACHAEL DORR *blogs about crafts at RachaelRabbit.blogspot.com. She loves to knit and sew and often takes advantage of reusing materials.*

Supplies

- Batting for an 85-inch by 90-inch full-size quilt, cotton
- Broadcloth or flannel for the backing, cotton, extra wide (108 inches), 2½ yards
- Cutting mat
- Fabric for quilt binding, cotton, 45 inches wide, ½ yard
- Pins
- Ruler
- Rotary cutter
- Scissors
- Sewing machine
- Shirts, cotton, men's long-sleeve, button-down, 12
- Thread for piecing (cotton) and for quilting

Prep the fabric

Look for a complementary combination of shirts. Here, serene white fabric allows the eye to rest between patterned, mostly pastel pieces.

1 WASH AND DRY. Launder all of the cotton shirts on a hot cycle, and tumble dry on high to avoid future shrinkage.

2 DISMANTLE THE SHIRTS. Cut the collar, yoke, and cuffs off, and cut down each seam to get one back panel, two front panels and two arm panels per shirt. Press each panel, and cut them into 5½-inch squares. You should be able to cut approximately 25 squares from each men's shirt and will need a total of 306 squares to complete the full-size quilt.

3 DESIGN THE QUILT. Lay out and arrange the squares in any pattern you like. The finished quilt measures 85 by 90 inches.

 tip **CHAIN-PIECE**

To save time and thread, use a chain-piecing technique to sew the quilt together. For more information, visit RachaelRabbit.blogspot.com.

Sew the quilt top together

With all of the pieces in place, the sewing begins. Use ¼-inch seam allowances for all of the seams.

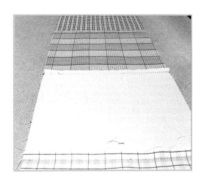

4 SEW THE STRIPS, AND PRESS. Sew 17 squares together to form a strip. Repeat for a total of 18 strips. Press all of the seams in the same direction.

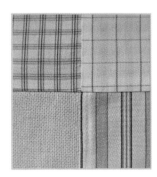

5 SEW THE QUILT TOP, AND PRESS. Sew the long edges of the strips together to create the quilt top. Make sure the seams align. Press the seams in the same direction.

Quilting diagrams

To bind the corners of your quilt quickly and neatly, follow the diagrams below.

Diagram 1

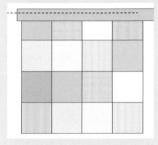

Diagram 2

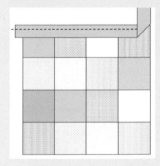

Diagram 3

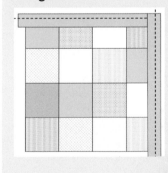

Layer and assemble the quilt

Now it's time to make the quilt super soft and warm by adding quilt batting and a flannel backing.

6 **LAYER AND PIN.** On a large, flat surface, lay the backing fabric wrong-side up first, and then layer the cotton batting. Add the quilt top right-side up. Smooth out all the layers; make sure that there are no wrinkles. From the center out, pin the layers together at least every 6 inches.

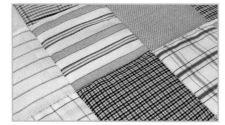

7 **QUILT "IN THE DITCH."** Finish the quilt in a simple, straight-stitch style. To do this, use a walking foot, and sew along the seam ditch of each square. For more quilting styles, see "Other quilting techniques" at right.

8 **CREATE A BORDER.** Cut nine, 2-inch-wide, 45-inch-long strips from the binding fabric. Sew all of the strips together to make one continuous piece of binding. Press all of the seams flat.

9 **START TO BIND THE QUILT.** Trim the quilt edges, and lay the binding right-side down, starting in the middle of one long edge. Attach the binding with a walking foot with a ½-inch seam allowance. Stop stitching ½-inch away from the corner.

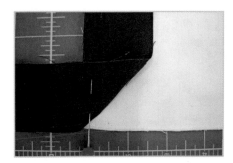

10 **BIND THE CORNERS.** Fold your binding up at a right angle, and pin it in place. Then, fold the binding down along the adjacent edge, and pin it in place. Sew the binding to the edge of your quilt, repeating these steps for each corner.

11 **FINISH THE BINDING.** On the back of the quilt, fold over the binding, and pin. Finish the binding with a blind/hem hand stitch.

Other quilting techniques

Tie the quilt. Use a strong thread or yarn to make a series of knots at regular intervals on the quilt.

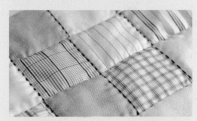

Hand-quilt. Start in the middle of the quilt, and sew along the edges of the squares. You can also sew across the squares or make other stitched patterns.

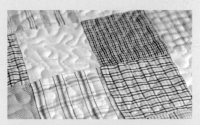

Free-motion quilt. Drop or cover your feed dogs, and use a darning foot, following either a stencil or an improvised pattern.

Embellish. For more visual interest, add appliqué patterns to the quilt squares.

Fall Foliage Rug

First, cut leaf shapes from faux suede—Ultrasuede for the luxe version or doe suede for an economical version. Then sew the leaves on a canvas backing for a nature-inspired throw rug. This project is quick to sew, but cutting the leaves does take some time. The results are worth it; this rug is luxurious under foot and handsome enough to hang on a wall. To speed the cutting process, you could use simple fabric strips or squares instead of leaf shapes.

Make it in your favorite autumnal color scheme or in spring greens. Just choose natural colors from your favorite season for a spectacular rug.

JUDITH NEUKAM *is the Executive Editor at* Threads.

Cut the leaves and prep the canvas

Determine your desired rug size, and calculate its area in square inches. Then use that measurement to create a grid on which you'll sew the leaves on every corner of each square.

Supplies

- Canvas
- Doe suede

Optional:
- Drop cloth
- Spray paint
- Ultra Suede
- Natural Suede

tip **MAKE IT A PARTY**

It's a job for one person to cut all those leaves—but invite a few friends over and it's an event. Just trace the leaves on the fabric's wrong side and give each person a pair of scissors.

Use scissors to cut the leaves from the suede.

Draw a grid on the right side of the canvas.

1 CUT THE LEAVES. Create your own leaf template by turning to nature for inspiration! We made ours with a simple maple design. Cut as many as you need (you can get 50 to 100 leaves from a yard of 60-inch-wide fabric, depending on design and spacing).

2 MARK THE CANVAS WITH A GRID. Determine how dense you want the rug. Draw a grid on the right side of the canvas the distance you want to position the leaves apart. On the rug shown, the leaves are 1½ inch apart. Then add a 2-inch-wide border for the hem. The finished rug shown is 36 inches by 47 inches, and it took 744 leaves to make it.

Sew on the leaves, and hem the edges

Turn and flip the leaves in various positions as you tack them to the canvas. Fold them in loose quarters so the bar-tack stitching goes through four layers. To freshen your rug, you can wash it and dry it in a dryer, but don't vacuum it, take it outside and shake it instead.

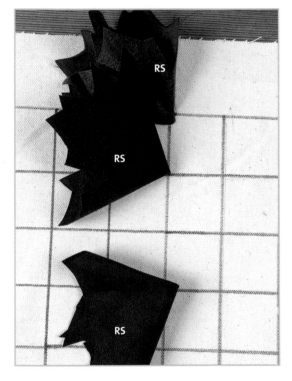

Bar-tack the leaves to the corners of the squares. Turn each leaf before you attach it so the shapes all look different. To vary appearance, fold a few wrong-side out occasionally, too.

3 **ATTACH THE LEAVES.** To attach a leaf to the corner of a square, pick up the leaf from the center of the right side, place it on the canvas, and bar-tack the point of fabric to the canvas, as shown at left. Turn the leaves in different directions when you bunch them.

tip **GET YOUR BEST PATTERN FROM NATURE**

Different leaf shapes create different looks. Study leaves around you and how they look on the ground. Also, study their color for inspiration. Maple, oak, elm, and beech are all great variations.

Turn over a new leaf

The rug shown here is doe suede, which is soft and washable. You can buy it at local fabric stores when it's in season, but it's available online year round. If you want to make a more deluxe version, here are some other options:

ULTRASUEDE
Like doe suede, Ultrasuede is hard-wearing, washable, and dryable, but it has more body, so the leaves will stand up more. It's narrower, so it will take about 30 percent more yardage to make as many leaves from it, and it can cost about 10 times as much. It's definitely a luxury touch.

REAL SUEDE, LEATHER, OR A COMBINATION
The most economical way to use real suede or leather is to purchase assembly-line scraps from a manufacturer or tanner. Natural suede does require professional cleaning, but a rug made of this material could be quite sturdy, depending on the weight of the skin.

4 HEM THE EDGES. To hem the edges, turn the canvas edges to the wrong side, and hand stitch. Or, apply a quality fabric glue to the border, turn the edge back, and press with your hands.

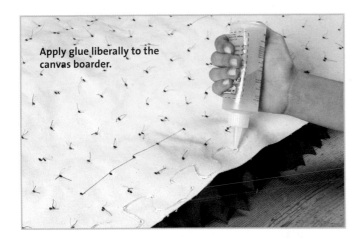

Apply glue liberally to the canvas boarder.

Turn the glued edge back with your hands, and press it in place.

Make it more realistic

Spray paints will adhere to the suede and withstand wear. Experiment with different effects and discover what a misting of paint does for your leaves.

Use spray paint to get a mottled effect that resembles the forest floor. On a newspaper or a drop cloth in your yard, scatter the leaves, creating two or even three layers; make the leaves overlap and touch. Then spray a sheer mist of gold, orange, yellow, or purple paint on the edges of the leaves (spray more than one color while you play Mother Nature, if you want). Let the paint dry, and then assemble your rug.

Stitched Lamp Shade

It's the little touches that make a room special. This simple project covers a lamp shade with pretty fabric and easy machine embroidery. It doesn't require much money, time, or effort. We'll show you how to measure a new or used lamp shade to create a pattern. After you cut and interface your fabric, you select and sew the embroidery motifs. Finishing is a breeze. Just edge the embroidered fabric with a satin stitch, and glue the new cover over the original.

This is a great project for leftover fabric. You can make lamp shades to match pillow or curtain projects. And since you did it yourself, you can add a soft glow of pride to your lighting scheme.

JENNIFER STERN-HASEMANN *is a contributor to* Threads. *Learn more about her work at JSternDesigns.com.*

Supplies

- Embroidery designs of your choice
- Embroidery thread
- Fabric (if you are layering over a patterned shade, pick fabric that won't allow the original to show through)
- Fusible interfacing
- Lamp shade (new or used)
- Metal binder clips
- Pattern paper
- Scissors
- Sewing machine with embroidery functions and hoop
- Spray adhesive (permanent)
- Tear-away stabilizer

Make a lamp shade pattern

Before you cut fabric to fit over your new or used lamp shade, you'll create a pattern. It is based on three simple measurements: the top and bottom circumferences and the vertical seam length.

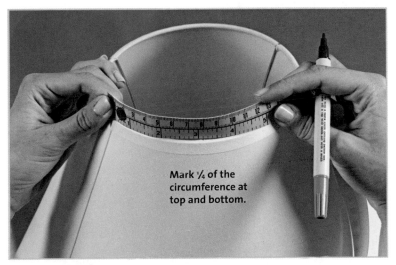

Mark ¼ of the circumference at top and bottom.

1 MEASURE THE LAMP SHADE'S TOP AND BOTTOM EDGES. If you're working with a new lamp shade, the diameters could be on the label. Multiply them by 3.14 to get the circumferences.

2 MARK ¼ THE CIRCUMFERENCE OF THE TOP AND BOTTOM EDGES. Divide by 4 the measurements you took in step 1. Start at the vertical seam, and mark the ¼ measurement along the top and bottom edges.

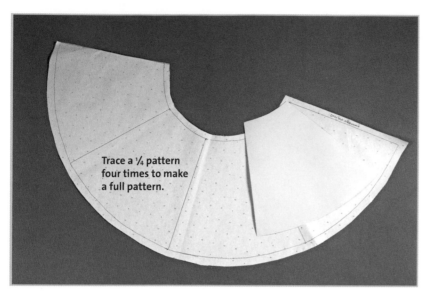

Trace a ¼ pattern
four times to make
a full pattern.

3 **MAKE A ¼ PATTERN.** Cut newsprint or pattern paper slightly larger than the ¼ area you marked. Smooth and wrap the paper over the lamp shade's edges. Trace the top and bottom edges. Remove the paper from the shade, and draw a seamline and a line connecting the top and bottom edge quarter marks. Trim the quarter pattern.

4 **MAKE A FULL PATTERN.** Trace and align the ¼ pattern four times to make a whole pattern. Add a ½-inch seam allowance to the complete pattern piece's edges. The seam allowance overlaps on the vertical seam and is trimmed on the top and bottom edges.

Embellish and apply the cover

Here's the most creative step—you get to select and stitch designs on the fabric. A few more actions finish the project—you wrap and glue the new cover to the lamp shade.

5 **CUT AND INTERFACE THE LAMP SHADE FABRIC.** Follow the pattern to cut fabric and interfacing. Fuse the interfacing to the fabric's entire wrong side.

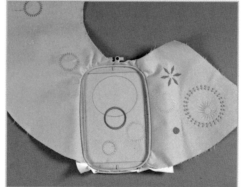

6 **EMBROIDER MOTIFS ONTO THE COVER.** Use tear- or wash-away stabilizer to support designs while stitching. Finish the top and bottom edges with satin stitching. Finish the vertical edge on one side. (It will overlap the unfinished vertical edge.)

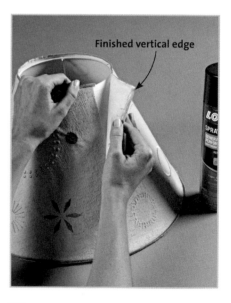

Finished vertical edge

7 **GLUE ON THE EMBROIDERED LAMP SHADE.** Use permanent spray adhesive. Smooth the embroidered lamp shade over the base shade in sections to minimize bubbles, and overlap the finished vertical edge over the unfinished edge.

Fabric Clocks

Contrary to what you might think, clocks are not complicated—at least, not the quartz mechanisms you can pick up at hobby and craft stores. They only seem like a mystery until you start playing with putting them into found objects. That's exactly how the idea for this fun little project came about!

This quick project lets you suit your décor with a result that's useful and unique. Clock mechanisms are easy to find and install. You can make clocks out of almost any object you can drill a hole through. A fabric-face clock cover is removable too, so you can wash or change it when you feel like it.

Fat quarters are used for this project because precut quilt fabric is inexpensive, easy to work with, and available in amazing colors and patterns—but there's no harm in using any fabric you choose! The clocks shown here have been made from flying disks, picnic bowls, and artist's canvases. Create your own clocks out of whatever suits your fancy!

SARAH MCFARLAND *is Editor at* Threads.

Supplies

- Bias tape (extra-wide, double-fold)
- Bodkin or safety pin
- Clock mechanism and hands
- Elastic cord
- Fabric, 1 fat quarter
- Fabric marker
- Flying disk
- Fray Check
- Fusible interfacing (a 2-inch square)
- Pencil
- Power drill
- Quilt batting, 1/4 yard
- Scissors
- Sewing machine
- Thread

Optional:
- Nail or round file to clean the clock shaft opening
- Spray paint for the clock hands

Create a fabric clock

A flying disk is the support for this cloth-covered clock face. This is a fun project for kids once an adult has done the prep work. The cloth faces can be made and swapped in a jiffy. Make new covers for holidays, birthdays, or any special event. If you want to add numbers, most clock mechanism kits come with them.

tip FIT THE FACE

Clock shafts come in different depths, from ¼ inch to 1 inch and beyond. If the clock shaft protrudes from the face, add a few washers between the clock works and the disk's wrong side.

Drill a hole in the disk.

1 MAKE A HOLE FOR THE CLOCK HANDS. Mark the center of your flying disk on the right side. Use a vise, or hold it firmly while you drill a center hole with a drill bit slightly larger than the clock shaft. Wear safety glasses, and drill over a work surface. Apply gentle pressure, and go slowly. Use a nail file to neaten or enlarge the hole.

Cut the fabric 2 inches from the line you traced.

Trace the disk shape on the fabric.

2 MEASURE THE CLOCK FABRIC. Mark the fat quarter's center on the wrong side. Drape the fabric, wrong side up, over the disk's convex side. Align the centers, and tuck the fabric around the disk's edges. Keep the fabric evenly draped and the centers aligned while you mark where the fabric begins to wrap under the edges, around the disk.

3 ADD A SEAM ALLOWANCE, AND CUT THE FABRIC. Remove the disk, and spread the fabric flat. Add 2 inches to the radius of the rough circle you traced around the disk. Cut out the larger circle. Cut a batting circle the size of the rough circle you traced.

Finish the clock face

Like a shower cap, the fabric circle is edged with elastic to keep it taut over the clock face. Cut a small hole for the clock shaft and the hands to come through the fabric.

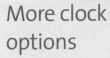

Pad the clock face with batting before you cover it.

4 ADD A CHANNEL FOR ELASTIC.
Slide the edge of the fabric into the center fold of the bias tape. Stitch close to the bias tape's inner edge; make sure to catch all the layers in the stitching. Overlap the bias tape ends about 1/2 inch when you complete the circle.

5 INSERT THE ELASTIC CORD. Use
the bodkin or a safety pin to run the elastic cord through the bias tape around the fabric edge. Place the batting circle over the disk's right side, and then cover with the fabric. Adjust so that the fabric center is aligned with the center hole. Pull the elastic taut on the disk's wrong side. Tie off, and trim the elastic.

Add hands to the shaft.

6 PREPARE TO ADD THE CLOCK
WORKS. With a craft knife, cut a tiny X through the fabric and batting at the disk center. Dritz® Fray Check™ and fusible interfacing should keep your fabric from raveling.

7 INSTALL THE CLOCK
MECHANISM AND HANDS. Spray-paint the hands if desired. Push the clock shaft through the holes. Follow the instructions that came with the clock mechanism to install it. Add the battery, and set the correct time.

More clock options

Once you have the basic idea, it's a cinch to experiment with different clock structures and cover treatments.

Turn a plastic bowl into a clock. Follow the same steps as for the flying disk clock. Just use the bowl upside down where the disk was right side up.

Cover an artist's canvas with fabric. This is a great way to make a rectangular clock. Choose where you want the clock shaft to come through; reinforce the canvas and the fabric at that point. Give your fabric a seam allowance generous enough to fold to the canvas' wrong side.

Trim and serge the fabric edges, then fold and staple it to the canvas back. Cut a hole for the clock mechanism through the fabric and canvas.

Make a four-part face. For a quilt-like look and seams at 3, 6, 9, and 12 o'clock, piece fabrics and center the clock shaft where the fabrics intersect.

Artful Pillows

Fresh and modern, these pillows of layered sheer fabrics juxtaposed with electric-colored zippers make unforgettable accents. Luckily, there's no need to run out to an upscale home décor shop to get them. Instead, head for your sewing machine. To get the color combination you want, test a variety of sheer fabrics together, and try laying them over white and over each other. The colors may end up coordinating with each other, showing through one another, or even creating a new color once combined. The fabric colors, plus straight seams and bright zippers, give the pillows a retro-modern feel. There are no rules for combining colors, so choose any that appeal to you. Feel free to vary the width of the stripes and to play around with the overlapping technique—experimenting with these fabrics is part of the fun!

LINDA BOSTON *is an artist and sewer in Woodbury, Connecticut. Visit her Web site at BostonPotandTile.com.*

Supplies

- Clear monofilament sewing thread
- Fusible spray, such as 606, for lightweight fabrics
- Invisible nylon zipper in a contrasting color, 20-inch
- Organza sheers in different colors, ½ yard of each
- Presscloth
- Square pillow form, 16-inch
- Rotary cutter, ruler, and mat
- White cotton broadcloth, ½ yard

Design with sheer layers

Start by cutting a white cotton cover for the pillow, then play with strips of sheers on the cover to create a design you love. Fold, overlap, and layer the sheers as desired to invent unique color combinations.

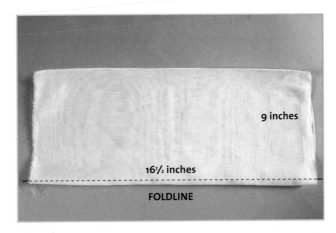

9 inches

16½ inches

FOLDLINE

1 FOR THE PILLOW COVER, cut a rectangle of white broadcloth 18 inches by 33 inches. Fold it in half crosswise, and lay it flat.

2 CUT 18-INCH BY 5-INCH STRIPS OF SHEER FABRICS. Be sure to cut exactly on-grain, to minimize raveling. Work with a rotary cutter to make the straightest, smoothest edges.

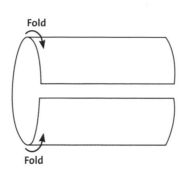

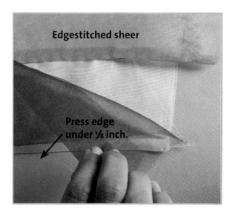

Edgestitched sheer

Press edge
under ⅛ inch.

3 **TEST THE STRIPS** on the white broadcloth square, layering and overlapping them to experiment with color combinations. Fold the long, cut edges of the strips under any width you like, to create darker bands of color. Be sure to include the contrasting zipper as part of your composition. When you're satisfied, transfer the sheers from the broadcloth by placing a sheet of fabric over the composition and carefully inverting it.

Fold

Fold

4 **FOLD THE BROADCLOTH COVER** so that the short ends are aligned at the center, where the zipper opening will be.

5 **FOLD AND PRESS ⅛ INCH TO THE RIGHT SIDE** along the short ends. Edgestitch the sheer strips in place on the pillow front, above and below the opening where the zipper will be sewn. Use a temporary spray adhesive to hold the strips in place.

Assemble the striped cover

Topstitch the contrasting zipper in place, then sew the pillow sides together for an easy, super-stylish home accessory.

6 **LAY THE ZIPPER ON THE COVER,** over the pressed edges, with the zipper's wrong side on the pillow cover. Leave an inch of zipper hanging off the ends of the pillow. Pin the zipper in place, baste it with hand stitches, or fuse it with narrow, fusible tape. Edgestitch the zipper with monofilament thread. Unzip the zipper about halfway.

Color combinations

Here are some tips for choosing colors —and a vibrant zipper.

• Work with an analogous color scheme and choose colors that are close together on the color wheel. For example, a red/pink/orange combination.

• Deepen colors by placing darker tones over lighter ones.

• Blend hues by placing lighter colors over darker ones.

• Choose a zipper color from across the color wheel: For example, a blue on red/orange scheme.

Close the pillow sides
with a French seam.

7 **SEW THE PILLOW CLOSED** with a french seam. With wrong sides together, sew the open ends of the cover closed, using a ⅜-inch seam allowance and stitching across the zipper at each end. Hold the zipper teeth close together at the open end as you sew. Trim the seam allowances to ¼ inch, and cut off the excess zipper ends. Turn the cover inside out, and resew the end seams, enclosing the raw seam allowances from the previous stitching.

8 **TURN THE COVER RIGHT-SIDE OUT,** and press as needed. Insert the pillow form, and zip the cover closed.

A Dashing Duvet

What better way to dress up a bedroom than with a new, sparkling duvet cover? It's an easy project that makes an impressive gift because you can personalize it with your own fabric selections. A duvet, by the way, is a soft comforter—with a removable cover—meant to eliminate the need for a top sheet or bedspread.

Here, you'll learn how to sew a patchwork duvet cover that has the easy charm of a patchwork quilt. The choice of fabrics—shimmery Indian silks, textured brocades—gives it the sophisticated edge of very expensive designer bedding. Your friend will think you spent a small fortune! He or she will never know that you used a combination of purchased cloth napkins, scraps from other projects, and a simple sheet for a backing—that is, unless you can't keep that delicious secret to yourself.

MARY RAY *is a contributing editor at* Threads.

FIRST MEASURE YOUR COMFORTER. The amount of fabric you will need for a duvet cover depends on the size of your comforter. Unfortunately, there aren't industry standards for comforters as there are with sheets and mattresses. So, you'll have to measure your comforter from edge to edge and end to end. Add 1-inch seam allowances to the side edges and to one end. Then add 2 inches to the other end to accommodate the closure.

To create the patchwork design shown here, all you really need to do is work within the above dimensions. Piecing can be a delightfully imprecise science. Just start sewing your napkins and scraps of fabric together in columns and, every once in a while, lay your columns over your comforter to check the fit. If you're a planner, you could divide your comforter measurements into sections, and plan your color placement exactly.

FINISH UP WITH DESIGNER TOUCHES. Before you start the step-by-step sewing process, finish the edges of each block and lattice strip with a serger or a zigzag stitch. This will keep the edges nice and neat and prevent fraying. Use snap tape for your closure. It's sturdy yet soft and invisible when snapped shut around your comforter. And, unlike hook-and-loop tape, it will never scratch your skin, or grab onto other fabrics in the washer and dryer.

Supplies

- Fabric scraps and cloth napkins
- Woolite® dye magnet
- Sharp scissors
- Sewing machine
- Thread
- Sheet for backing
- Snap tape
- Comforter

Sew the blocks together

Before you begin, test your fabrics for colorfastness by rubbing a damp, warm washcloth over the back of each fabric. If one bleeds, and it's washable, prewash it using a dye magnet; otherwise, dry-clean the piece.

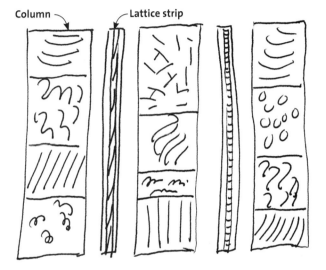

Column   Lattice strip

1 SEW THE BLOCKS IN COLUMNS. For the large-block scheme here, there's no set formula. Simply sew your blocks, right sides together, to create columns. Press the seam allowances open.

2 ADD LATTICE STRIPS. Cut strips of striped fabric the length of the duvet and 3 to 5 inches wide, plus seam allowances. Sew them between the columns. Press the seam allowances open.

Continued on next page

tip   **AN IMPRECISE SCIENCE**

The column widths and block heights should vary for visual appeal.

Choosing fabrics

Channel your inner designer: selecting and mixing fabrics is more than half the fun! Go bold, girly, or classic.

CONSIDER END USE
The types of fabric you should choose depend on how the duvet will be used. If it will be a substitute for a top sheet, you'll want smooth, light fabric such as quilter's cotton that's comfortable next to your skin. If your duvet will be more decorative such as the one at left, you have more options: silk dupioni, taffeta, or brocade. If the duvet will have to stand up to rowdy kids or pets, opt for easy-to-wash, sturdy fabrics such as denim, corduroy, and twills.

RAID YOUR STASH
There really are no rules with this duvet cover, so start with fabric pieces you have left over from other projects. Just choose colors, textures, and patterns that speak to you and work well together. Then head to a local department or home store, and buy a bunch of cloth napkins. Sew them together for a great patchwork look with the added bonus of not needing to finish the seams!

MIX AND MATCH
Narrow down your fabric choices to ten to fifteen. Make sure that they're comparable in weight, but don't be afraid to mix prints, stripes, plaids, and textures. Think about color! For this duvet, orange is the base color, and ocean blues and greens are accents.

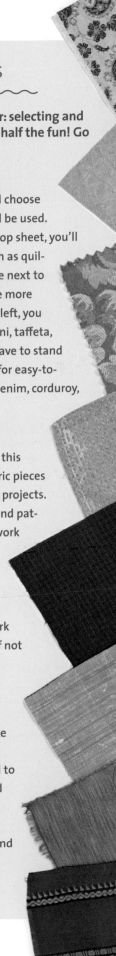

Back

Wrong side

Optional corner openings

3 ATTACH THE BACK. Depending on the duvet size and the width of the fabric you use, you may need to first piece the back, as shown at left. The duvet then goes together like a big pillowcase. Pin the top to the back, right sides together. Sew around three sides with a 1-inch seam. Leave the top end open.

4 ADD SNAP-TAPE CLOSURE. First make a double hem at the top edge: Turn in 1 inch, press, turn again, and press. Machine-stitch close to the inside fold. With wrong sides together, pin the back and front together at the top, and sew across 10 inches from each side seam. Open the snap tape, and machine-sew one side to each open edge.

TIP: If you don't have snap tape on hand, make tie closures. Cut 14x3-inch fabric strips. (You'll need enough pairs to cover the opening when spaced about 10 inches apart.) With right sides together, fold each tie in half lengthwise. Sew along the long side and one short end. Turn, press, and then sew them on the inside of the duvet opening.

tip **LEAVE CORNER OPENINGS**

To simplify dressing your comforter, add this feature. Leave a small 5-inch opening at each corner of the closed end of the duvet cover. These peepholes let you reach in and pull your comforter into place. No more struggles!

When you attach the back in step 3 at left, leave each long end open 5 inches at the bottom corners. Press the seams open. Then create a narrow hem in the openings: turn in the edges of the seam allowances ¼ inch. Machine-stitch around the openings to secure.

Tablecloth Curtain

If you are considering new window-treatment options, here is a little decorating advice: Use what you love. Raid your linen closet or local thrift shop for vintage tablecloths and create unique curtains in different styles and sizes for the kitchen or any room in the house. If the tablecloth is fragile, supplement older material with newer, stronger background fabrics to support the more delicate materials from the past. Here, the two layers join only at the top, which makes them come together more quickly, and gives the curtain a light, breezy quality.

JENNIE ARCHER ATWOOD *Excerpted from "Pairing Vintage and New Fabrics" in* Threads *issue no. 102*

Supplies

- Fabric, amount determined by desired curtain size
- Ribbon, 1-inch-wide, 12-inch-long strips
- Scissors
- Sewing machine
- Tablecloth, vintage
- Thread

Prep the tablecloth and underlayer

Part of the charm of vintage textiles is their imperfection. Check your tablecloth (or vintage linen) for worn spots, stains, and rips. You may need to use a little elbow grease to get it into its best condition.

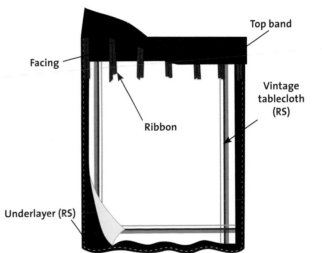

Top band
Facing
Ribbon
Vintage tablecloth (RS)
Underlayer (RS)

1 CUT THE TABLECLOTH TO SIZE. Hold the tablecloth up to the window, and fold excess fabric over at the top to adjust its length. After you have achieved the desired length, cut the excess fabric off 5 inches below the fold at the top of the tablecloth.

2 CUT THE UNDERLAYER. Measure the width and length of the cut tablecloth. Cut the underlayer 7 inches wider and 4 inches longer than the tablecloth.

3 CUT THE TOP BAND AND ITS FACING. To determine the length, subtract 3 inches from the width of the underlayer, and cut two 6-inch-wide bands that long from the same fabric you used for the underlayer. One is the top band, and the other is the top-band facing.

tip **MAKE IT A PAIR**

Sew one curtain or two. Here, we make a single curtain panel. But for a different look, cut your tablecloth and underlayer to make two curtains, and hang them side by side.

Hem the edges

Hem the sides of the underlayer. If you trimmed the edges of your tablecloth, you'll have to hem it as well.

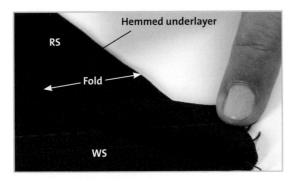

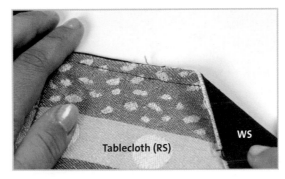

6 POSITION THE TOP BAND. Lay the band wrong side up across the top of the tablecloth. Stitch all three layers together across the top edge with a ½-inch seam allowance.

4 HEM THE UNDERLAYER. On each edge except the top, fold the fabric 1 inch to the wrong side, and then fold again along the raw edge. Press, and sew.

5 ALIGN THE UNDERLAYER WITH THE TABLECLOTH. Lay the underlayer right side up on your work surface. Place the tablecloth right side up on top of it, and align the top edges.

Add ribbon ties

After you've sewn the three layers together, sew the ribbons to the free top-band edge. Use them to attach the finished curtain to either the rod or curtain rings.

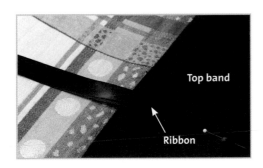

9 SEW THE EDGES. Align the band with the curtain/band seam, lay the facing wrong side up on top of the top band, and align the sides and top edges. Sew a ½-inch seam allowance up the sides and across the top edges through all the layers, catching the ribbon folds in the seams, as shown at right.

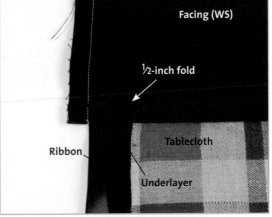

7 PRESS THE TOP-BAND FACING. Press one long side ½ inch to the wrong side.

8 BASTE THE TIES IN PLACE. Cut 12-inch-long ribbon strips for the ties. Fold each in half, pin them evenly spaced across the band's top edge, and baste them in place.

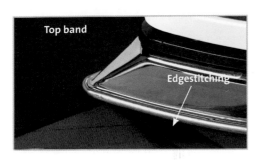

10 TURN THE FACING AND PRESS. Turn the facing right side out, exposing the ties. Then, press the top band.

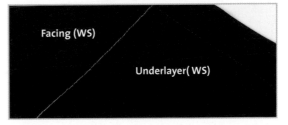

11 EDGESTITCH THE FACING TO THE UNDERLAYER. Fold the tablecloth and ties out of the way, and edgestitch the lower edge of the facing to the underlayer.

Designer Sheers

Summer is the perfect time to transform those plain, old curtains into a designer focal point.

You can make gorgeous embroidered sheer panels designed just the way you want them right at home. Pick a design that goes with your home décor; then let your embroidery machine do all the work. With a little planning, you can set it on autopilot, and watch some beautiful designs emerge.

JENNIFER STERN-HASEMANN *is a contributor to* Threads. *Learn more about her work at JSternDesigns.com.*

"Balloonflower" is one of the many designs available at EmbroideryOnline.com.

Supplies

- Lightweight cotton batiste or silk organza (amount determined by your window size)
- Embroidery design of your choice
- Printed templates for placement
- Coordinating embroidery thread
- Spray starch
- Wash-away stabilizer
- Temporary adhesive spray
- Embroidery machine
- Scissors

Make sheer curtains

Creating designer-style curtains is easier than you think it is. Start by finding fabric: choose lightweight cotton batiste for a casual look or silk organza for a more elegant effect. Check out home-decorating fabrics for a better color selection.

1 DETERMINE THE LENGTH AND WIDTH OF THE PANELS. For the length, measure from the curtain rod down to where you want your sheers to fall. If you plan to use a standard curtain rod, add to your measurement 3½ inches for a casing and 4 inches for a hem. For the width, measure across your window from one outside edge of the window molding to the other; multiply that measurement by 2½. If you're making two panels for your window, divide the result by two. Then add 2 inches for side hems.

2 WASH AND DRY THE FABRIC IN GENTLE CYCLE. Use the same method to launder your finished curtains. After washing, lay the fabric on your ironing board, spray it with starch, and then press.

3 CUT OUT THE PANELS. Use the dimensions you determined when you measured your window in step 1.

4 HEM THE SIDE EDGES. Turn the side edges under ½ inch, and press well. Turn the folded edge under an additional ½ inch to encase the raw edge. Press well, and pin it in place. Using a 3mm stitch length, edgestitch along the inside fold to secure the hem.

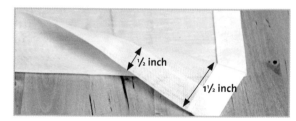

5 TURN THE TOP OF EACH PANEL UNDER. Turn the top edge under ½ inch, and press. Turn it under again 1½ inch, press well, and pin it in place. Stitch along the inside fold to form the bottom of the casing, and then stitch ½ inch from the top edge to finish the casing and make the ruffle.

6 MAKE THE HEM. Turn the bottom edge under 2 inches, and press well. Turn the folded edge under 2 more inches to encase the raw edge. Press well, and pin it in place. Use a 3mm stitch length to edgestitch the upper fold.

Embroider your designs

Now that your sheers are sewn, it's time to make them stand out. Make this as simple or elaborate as you wish: choose an embroidery design you can repeat along the hem and inside edge, or position it in a random pattern as we did here. With a little planning, your sheers will rival the ones in your favorite catalog.

Template

7 **USE YOUR EMBROIDERY SOFTWARE.** Combine as many individual designs as will fit in your largest hoop. Save each combination as a single embroidery design, and print a template use as your guide. Mark each design's position with a wash-away marker.

8 **IMPORT EMBROIDERY DESIGNS INTO YOUR SEWING MACHINE.** When you've finished, wind a bobbin with the same thread you'll be using in the needle. This keeps the back of your curtain looking just as nice as the front. Place wash-away stabilizer in the hoop. Spray the stabilizer with temporary adhesive.

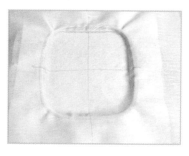

9 **POSITION THE FABRIC IN THE HOOP.** Use the placement lines as a guide. Smooth the fabric firmly against the tacky stabilizer.

10 **STITCH YOUR DESIGN.** Repeat the process until you've embroidered the curtain according to your design.

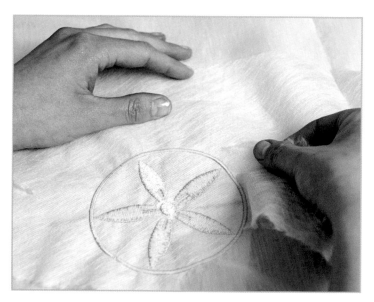

11 **REMOVE THE STABILIZER.** Gently tear away as much wash-away stabilizer as you can from around the edges of the embroidery. Then wash your curtains to remove the remaining stabilizer, marks, and spray starch.

tip **TAME YOUR SHEER FABRICS**

Spray starch adds stability and body. It also makes placing and embroidering designs easier.

Look for these other *Threads* Selects booklets at www.tauntonstore.com and wherever crafts are sold.

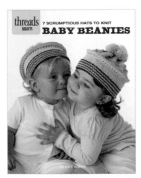

Baby Beanies
Debby Ware

EAN: 9781621137634
8 ½ x 10 ⅞, 32 pages
Product# 078001
$9.95 U.S., $11.95 Can.

Fair Isle Flower Garden
Kathleen Taylor

EAN: 9781621137702
8 ½ x 10 ⅞, 32 pages
Product# 078008
$9.95 U.S., $11.95 Can.

**Fair Isle Hats,
Scarves, Mittens & Gloves**
Kathleen Taylor

EAN: 9781621137719
8 ½ x 10 ⅞, 32 pages
Product# 078009
$9.95 U.S., $11.95 Can.

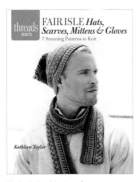

Lace Socks
Kathleen Taylor

EAN: 9781621137894
8 ½ x 10 ⅞, 32 pages
Product# 078012
$9.95 U.S., $11.95 Can.

Colorwork Socks
Kathleen Taylor

EAN: 9781621137740
8 ½ x 10 ⅞, 32 pages
Product# 078011
$9.95 U.S., $11.95 Can.

**DIY Bride Cakes &
Sweets**
Khris Cochran

EAN: 9781621137665
8 ½ x 10 ⅞, 32 pages
Product# 078004
$9.95 U.S., $11.95 Can.

**DIY Bride Beautiful
Bouquets**
Khris Cochran

EAN: 9781621137672
8 ½ x 10 ⅞, 32 pages
Product# 078005
$9.95 U.S., $11.95 Can.

Bead Necklaces
Susan Beal

EAN: 9781621137641
8 ½ x 10 ⅞, 32 pages
Product# 078002
$9.95 U.S., $11.95 Can.

Drop Earrings
Susan Beal

EAN: 9781621137658
8 ½ x 10 ⅞, 32 pages
Product# 078003
$9.95 U.S., $11.95 Can.

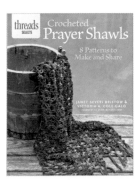

Crocheted Prayer Shawls
Janet Severi Bristow &
Victoria A. Cole-Galo

EAN: 9781621137689
8 ½ x 10 ⅞, 32 pages
Product# 078006
$9.95 U.S., $11.95 Can.

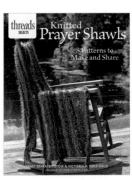

Knitted Prayer Shawls
Janet Severi Bristow &
Victoria A. Cole-Galo

EAN: 9781621137696
8 ½ x 10 ⅞, 32 pages
Product# 078007
$9.95 U.S., $11.95 Can.

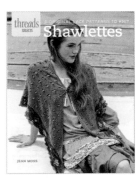

Shawlettes
Jean Moss

EAN: 9781621137726
8 ½ x 10 ⅞, 32 pages
Product# 078010
$9.95 U.S., $11.95 Can.

Easy-to-Sew Flowers
EAN: 9781621138259
8 ½ x 10 ⅞, 32 pages
Product# 078017
$9.95 U.S., $9.95 Can.

Easy-to-Sew Gifts
EAN: 9781621138310
8 ½ x 10 ⅞, 32 pages
Product# 078023
$9.95 U.S., $9.95 Can.

Easy-to-Sew Handbags
EAN: 9781621138242
8 ½ x 10 ⅞, 32 pages
Product# 078016
$9.95 U.S., $9.95 Can.

Easy-to-Sew Kitchen
EAN: 9781621138327
8 ½ x 10 ⅞, 32 pages
Product# 078024
$9.95 U.S., $9.95 Can.

Easy-to-Sew Lace
EAN: 9781621138228
8 ½ x 10 ⅞, 32 pages
Product# 078014
$9.95 U.S., $9.95 Can.

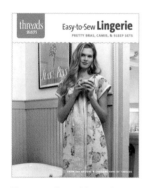

Easy-to-Sew Lingerie
EAN: 9781621138235
8 ½ x 10 ⅞, 32 pages
Product# 078015
$9.95 U.S., $9.95 Can.

Easy-to-Sew Pet Projects
EAN: 9781621138273
8 ½ x 10 ⅞, 32 pages
Product# 078018
$9.95 U.S., $9.95 Can.

Easy-to-Sew Pillows
EAN: 9781621138266
8 ½ x 10 ⅞, 32 pages
Product# 078019
$9.95 U.S., $9.95 Can.

**Easy-to-Sew
Scarves & Belts**
EAN: 9781621138211
8 ½ x 10 ⅞, 32 pages
Product# 078013
$9.95 U.S., $9.95 Can.

Easy-to-Sew Skirts
EAN: 9781621138280
8 ½ x 10 ⅞, 32 pages
Product# 078020
$9.95 U.S., $9.95 Can.

Easy-to-Sew Tote Bags
EAN: 9781621138297
8 ½ x 10 ⅞, 32 pages
Product# 078021
$9.95 U.S., $9.95 Can.

Easy-to-Sew Windows
EAN: 9781621138303
8 ½ x 10 ⅞, 32 pages
Product# 078022
$9.95 U.S., $9.95 Can.

Prairie Girl Gifts
Jennifer Worick

EAN: 9781621139492
8 1/2 x 10 7/8, 32 pages
Product # 078030
$9.95 U.S., $9.95 Can.

Bead Bracelets
Susan Beal

EAN: 9781621139515
8 1/2 x 10 7/8, 32 pages
Product# 078028
$9.95 U.S., $9.95 Can.

Quick Crochet Tops
Afya Ibomu

EAN: 9781621139546
8 1/2 x 10 7/8, 32 pages
Product# 078025
$9.95 U.S., $9.95 Can.

Learn to Crochet
Afya Ibomu

EAN: 9781621139539
8 1/2 x 10 7/8, 32 pages
Product# 078026
$9.95 U.S., $9.95 Can.

Prairie Girl Sewing
Jennifer Worick

EAN: 9781621139508
8 1/2 x 10 7/8, 32 pages
Product# 078029
$9.95 U.S., $9.95 Can.

Cable Shawlettes
Jean Moss

EAN: 9781621137733
8 1/2 x 10 7/8, 32 pages
Product# 078037
$9.95 U.S., $9.95 Can.

Felted Scarves, Hats & Mittens
Kathleen Taylor

EAN: 9781627100960
8 1/2 x 10 7/8, 32 pages
Product # 078031
$9.95 U.S., $9.95 Can.

Dog Coats & Collars
Sally Muir and Joanna Osborne

EAN: 9781627100984
8 1/2 x 10 7/8, 32 pages
Product# 078033
$9.95 U.S., $9.95 Can.

Pet Projects to Knit
Sally Muir and Joanna Osborne

EAN: 9781627100991
8 1/2 x 10 7/8, 32 pages
Product# 078034
$9.95 U.S., $9.95 Can.

Socktopus Socks
Alice Yu

EAN: 9781627101004
8 1/2 x 10 7/8, 32 pages
Product# 078035
$9.95 U.S., $9.95 Can.

Favorite Felted Gifts to Knit
Kathleen Taylor

EAN: 9781627101653
8 1/2 x 10 7/8, 32 pages
Product# 078038
$9.95 U.S., $9.95 Can.

Small Projects to Quilt
Joan Ford

EAN: 9781627100977
8 1/2 x 10 7/8, 32 pages
Product# 078032
$9.95 U.S., $9.95 Can.

Credits

Many of the projects, patterns, and photos in this booklet have appeared previously in issues of *Threads, SewStylish,* and/or *CraftStylish*. Listed here are the author, photographer, and *Threads* issue # or publication title.

Cotton Shirt Quilt

Rachael Dorr. Process photos: Rachael Dorr. All other photos: Sloan Howard. Stylist: Kayte Terry. *CraftStylish*, Vol. VI

Fall Foliage Rug

Judith Neukam. Photos: Sloan Howard. Stylist: Jessica Saal. *SewStylish*, Winter 2009

Stitched Lamp Shade

Jennifer Stern-Hasemann. Photos: Sloan Howard. Stylist: Jessica Saal. *SewStylish*, Winter 2010

Fabric Clocks

Sarah McFarland. Photos: Sloan Howard. *SewStylish*, Winter 2010

Artful Pillows

Linda Boston. Photos: Sloan Howard. Stylist: Jessica Saal. *SewStylish*, Winter 2010

A Dashing Duvet

Mary Ray. Photos: Scott Phillips. Stylist: Jessica Saal. Illustrations: Mary Ray. *SewStylish*, Holiday 2007

Tablecloth Curtain

Excerpted from Threads article "Pairing Vintage and New Fabrics" by Jennie Archer Atwood. Photos: Sloan Howard. Stylist: Jessica Saal. Illustrations: Kat Riehle. *Threads* #102

Designer Sheers

Jennifer Stern-Hasemann. Photos: Zach Desart and Burcu Avsar. Process Photos: Sloan Howard. *CraftStylish*, Quick Stuff to Make, Summer 2008